Benevolence Towards Parents

Ibn Qayyim Al-Jawziyya

Translated & Comments by Al Reshah

Alreshah.net

Canada

Copyright © 2018 by **Alreshah**

All rights reserved. No part of this publication may be reproduced, distributed or transmitted in any form or by any means, without prior written permission.

AlReshah
www.Alreshah.net

Publisher's Note: This is translation of book without change of meaning as best as the translator could achieve with few comments in the footnote to clarify If any error is found please contact us through our website alreshah.net.

Book Layout © 2017 BookDesignTemplates.com

Benevolence towards Parents/ Ibn Qayyim Al-Jawziyya. -- 1st ed.
ISBN 978-1-7753434-1-7

Gifted to my Parents ………

Thanks for:
Stacey Con
Dawn Birdsong Vadbunker
Fox Buck

For their input and review of this Translation

Please note: this book also includes a collection of Hadiths the Imam his soul rest in peace didn't mention the source or the strength of the Hadith, as part of Translation in the footnote I cited the source and if the Hadith is weak or rejected by Scholars of Hadith I also note that.

Footnotes: Mohammad Ahmad

Contents

Introduction 1

Fostering Filial Benevolence and Kinship Ties In Light Of Reason 3

Fostering Filial Benevolence and Kinship Ties In Light Of God's Ordinance 7

Fostering Filial Benevolence in Light Of Sunnah 11

The Precedence of The Mother in Benevolence 19

The Reward for Benevolence Towards Parents 27

Ultimate Benevolence Towards Parents 31

The Sin of Being Undutiful Towards Parents 37

Connecting with Parents After Their Death 55

The Reward of Fostering Ties Of Kinship And The Punishment For Severing It 63

• CHAPTER 1 •

Introduction

In the Name of Allah, the All-Merciful, Most Merciful

The humble servant of God who seeks to be blessed with His mercy, the distinguished scholar, al-imam Jamalud-Din, Abu al-Faraj, 'Abdul Rahman ibn Ali ibn Muhammad ibn al-Jawzi, may God bestow upon us the benefit of his knowledge, Amen: Praise be to Allah who enjoins man to be righteous and forbids him from being undutiful; His blessings and peace be on our master Muhammad, the most truthful and honest, and on his kinsfolk and followers on the Day of Absolute Justice.

I have witnessed the disregard which some of the youth of our time have demonstrated towards filial benevolence and their failure to conceive it as a fundamental article of religion. They yell at their parents, ignoring their duty of being obedient towards them and severing the ties of kinship that God Almighty has emphatically ordained to foster and has strictly forbidden to sever. This severance may be even coupled with abandonment and displayed with explicitness. They also refrain from solacing the poor with what God has endowed them, seemingly doubting the reward for their act of charity. They hold up their favors presuming, deluded as they are, they are no longer favors, neither in light of reason nor the Islamic Law. All such things are endorsed by reason and are recompensed with bountiful rewards or incur severe punishment as stated in the Quran and Sunnah.

Accordingly, the main objective of my book is to ring a bell to arouse the absentminded and remind the steadfast. I have divided it into seamless chapters and sections; may Allah endow this work with His guidance and support.

• CHAPTER 2 •

Fostering Filial Benevolence and Kinship Ties In Light Of Reason

Any reasonable human being recognizes, beyond doubt, the benefaction of the Creator and likewise the benefaction of parents on man. The mother has endured various difficulties and hard times during the process of pregnancy and labor. After giving birth, she has provided him with excess care, stayed awake at night to ensure his protection, renounced her desires, and gave him total precedence over herself.

Similarly, the father, who is the cause of his son's existence, has bestowed him with his benevolence and compassion, and afforded his nurture and general well-being.

Ibn Qayyim Al-Jawziyya

So, a sound person acknowledges the favors of the benefactor and strives to reward him, whereas a mean person demerit the favors that were bestowed on him and reciprocates them with ingratitude and evil payoff. Needless to say that however hard a benevolent son endeavors to repay his parents, it will never suffice their due gratitude.

It was narrated that Zara'a ibn Ibrahim said that a man came to Omar[1], may Allah be pleased with him and said, "I have a mother so old and weakened that I carry her all around: whenever she needs to relieve herself or perform her ablution while I turn my face away. Have I discharged my duty towards her? Omar said, 'No!'

The man argued, 'Didn't I carry her on my back and dedicated myself to her service?' So, Omar said, 'She was doing this out of genuine love and care for your survival and well-being, whereas you are doing this wishing she were dead.'

Omar, may Allah be pleased with him, saw a man carrying his mother like a corpse on his back during tawaf [a worship ritual of pilgrimage] and saying,

I bear my mother as she had borne me — and breast-fed me milk and sympathy Omar, moved by the man's words, said,

---

[1] Omar Bin Khattab – RA- was one of the most powerful and influential Muslim caliphs in history. He was a senior companion of the Prophet Muhammad PBUH. He succeeded Abu Bakr as the second caliph.

BENEVOLENCE TOWARDS PARENTS

"Indeed I would have given up the world if I could ever get reunited with my mother and tend her with all due care."

Another man told Abdulah ibn Omar[2] (may Allah be pleased with them both), "I carried my mother on my back from Khurasan till she accomplished the pilgrimage rituals. Have I thus repaid her favors? Abdulah said, 'No, not even a single pang of childbirth.'"

In a similar manner, man is ordained to extend his help and benevolence to other relatives and kinship and never neglect his duty in this respect.

---

[2] the son of the second Caliph Umar and a brother-in-law and companion of the Islamic prophet Muhammad PBUH. He was a prominent authority in hadith and law.

• CHAPTER 3 •

Fostering Filial Benevolence and Kinship Ties In Light Of God's Ordinance

God had said, Exalted is he, "وَقَضَىٰ رَبُّكَ أَلَّا تَعْبُدُوا إِلَّا إِيَّاهُ وَبِالْوَالِدَيْنِ إِحْسَانًا إِمَّا يَبْلُغَنَّ عِندَكَ الْكِبَرَ أَحَدُهُمَا أَوْ كِلَاهُمَا فَلَا تَقُل لَّهُمَا أُفٍّ وَلَا تَنْهَرْهُمَا وَقُل لَّهُمَا قَوْلًا كَرِيمًا (٢٣) وَاخْفِضْ لَهُمَا جَنَاحَ الذُّلِّ مِنَ الرَّحْمَةِ وَقُل رَّبِّ ارْحَمْهُمَا كَمَا رَبَّيَانِي صَغِيرًا"

(And your Lord has decreed that you not worship except Him, and to parents, good treatment. Whether one or both of them reach old age [while] with you, say not to them [so much as], "uff," and do not repel them but speak to them a noble word. (23) And lower to them the wing of humility out of mercy and say, "My Lord, have mercy upon them as they brought me up [when I was] small." (24))[3]

Abu Bakr ibn al-Anbari stated (this decree is not a matter of ruling inasmuch as it is a decisive command and mandatory obligation. The word 'ordained' in language implies cutting something with definitude and precision).

(And that you must be kind to your parents): signifies benevolence and bountifulness. Ibn Abbas stated, "Do not shake off your attire in front of them lest the dust should annoy them."

(Never say 'Ugh or uff' to them): 'ugh' implies five meanings: the first implies the dirt under the nail, according to al-Khalil; the second implies the dirt of the ear, according to al-Assma'i; the third implies the snip of a nail, according to Tha'lab; the fourth implies contempt and belittlement, according to Ibn al-Anbari; and the fifth implies what you lift from the ground such as sticks or reeds, according to Ibn Fares.

I have related to our linguistics scholar Abi Mansour that 'ugh' means foul-smelling. It is basically derived from huffing which aims to brush off dust and other tiny particles, hence it is generally used to indicate insignificant things.

(Or chide them): don't raise your voice or use words which suggest your being bored or bothered with them.

'Ataa ibn Abi Rabah said, "Do not dab with your hand at them."

---

[3] Al-Isra 17:23-24

BENEVOLENCE TOWARDS PARENTS

(But always speak gently and kindly to them): i.e., address them gently with the nicest expression. Saeed bin al-Musayyib said: like the speech of a guilty slave addressing a harsh master.

(And spread over them humbly the wings of your tenderness): offer them your mercy and compassion.

(Be grateful to Me and to your parents): in order to emphasize the rights of parents, God has linked His praise to theirs.

• CHAPTER 4 •

Fostering Filial Benevolence in Light Of Sunnah

It was narrated that Mu'adh ibn Jabal said: The Messenger of Allah (peace be upon him) told me, "Do not disobey your parents, even if they order you to abandon your family and property."

Ahmad said: Yahya told me, according to Ibn Abi Ze'eb, according to his uncle Al-Harith, according to Dumra, as stated by Abdulah ibn Omar (may Allah be pleased with them) said, "I was married to a woman whom Omar hated, so he advised me to divorce her but I refused. So, Omar went to the Prophet, peace be upon him, who eventually told me, "Obey your father!"

It was narrated that 'Obada ibn as-Samit said: The Prophet (peace be upon him) said, "Do not disobey your parents even if they ordered you to give up the whole world." It was also narrated that Jabir said that the Messenger of Allah (peace be upon him) stated, "Impart your benevolence onto your parents so your children may impart theirs onto you."

Zayd ibn Ali ibn al-Hussayn told his son Yahya: "God, Exalted is He, was not content to entrust me to your care, so He urged you to take care of me; meanwhile, He was content to entrust you to my care, so He did not urge me to take care of you."

Giving precedence to filial benevolence over Jihad and Hijrah

Abdulah ibn Amr (may Allah be pleased with them both) related, "A man came pledging allegiance to the Prophet (peace be upon him) saying: I came to pledge allegiance to you to immigrate and I left my parents crying. The Prophet said, "Go back and make them laugh just as you made them cry."[4]

It was also narrated that Abu Sa'eed al-Khudri said: a man migrated to the Prophet (peace be upon him) from Yemen, so the Prophet asked him, "Are your parents in Yemen?" The man said, "Yes." The Prophet asked, "Did they grant you permission to migrate?" He said, "No." So the Prophet instructed him, "Go back to your parents and ask their permission; otherwise, keep their company and show your benevolence to them."[5]

---

[4] Al-Bukhari and Muslim
[5] Sunan Abi Dawud

BENEVOLENCE TOWARDS PARENTS

On the authority of Ibn Abbas that he said: a woman came accompanied by her son who wanted to join jihad (fight for the cause of God), but she forbade him. The Prophet (peace be upon him) said, "Reside with your parents and you will have the same reward that you desire."

It was narrated that Abdulah ibn Amr (may Allah be pleased with them both) said: a man came to the Prophet (peace be upon him) to ask permission for jihad. The Prophet asked him, "Is anyone of your parents still living?" He said, "My mother." So, the Prophet said, "Go back to her and bestow your benevolence on her." [6]The man went out to prepare the riding camel for departure, so the Prophet said, "God's satisfaction is linked to the parents' satisfaction."

The most pleasing deed for God is benevolence towards parents

It was narrated that Abu Amr al-Shaibani said: the owner of this dwelling, referring to Abdulah ibn Mas'ud, told us: I asked the Messenger of God (peace be upon him), "Which deed is the most pleasing for God?" The Prophet said, "Performing prayers

---

[6] In Al-Bukhari and Muslim- 'Abdullah bin 'Umar (RAA) narrated 'A man came to the Messenger of Allah (PBUH) asking his permission to go out for Jihad. The Messenger of Allah (PBUH) asked him, "Are your parents alive?" He replied, 'Yes.' The Messenger of Allah (PBUH) then said to him, "Then your Jihad would be with them (i.e. in looking after them and being at their service.)."

in their due time." I said: "Then what?" He said, "Benevolence towards parents." I said, "Then what?" He said: "Jihad (fight) for the cause of God."[7]

Benevolence grants Divine blessing to one's life

On the authority of Sahl ibn Mu'adh, on the authority of his father, that he said: The Prophet (peace be upon him) said, "Blessed is he who shows benevolence towards his parents and his life is endowed with Divine grace."[8]

It was narrated that Abu Sa'eed al-Khudri and Abu Hurayrah said that the Prophet (peace be upon him) said, "O son of Adam, should you be benevolent towards your parents and foster ties of kinship, God will facilitate your affairs and prolong your life. Obey your Lord to be counted with the wise and do not disobey Him and be counted with the ignorant."

It was narrated by Salman that he said: The Prophet (peace be upon him) said, "Nothing except benevolence prolongs one's life."

On authority of Thawban.

It was narrated that Anas (may Allah be pleased with him) said: The Prophet (peace be upon him) said, "Whoever wants to enjoy a long and blessed life and multiply his wealth, let him show benevolence towards his parents and foster the ties of his kinship."

---

[7] Sunan an-Nasa'i
[8] Al-Adab Al-Mufrad

BENEVOLENCE TOWARDS PARENTS

How to show benevolence towards parents

Benevolence entails willingness to obey their orders unless such orders are religiously prohibited. Moreover, their orders should have precedence over works of supererogation. Benevolence also entails shunning what they forbade, spending on them, fulfilling their desires, taking extra care of them, being courteous and respectful towards them, speaking gently without yelling or looking at them straight in the face, avoid calling them with their plain names, walking behind them, and forbearing with patience what occurs from them which is hateful to him."

I heard Talq ibn Ali saying: The Prophet (peace be upon him) once said, "If I could rejoin with my parents or one of them and I started my prayer, reciting al-Fatiha and one of my parents called, "O Muhammad!", I would immediately reply, "Here I am at your service."[9]

On the authority of Abu Ghassan al-Dabbi that he went out walking while his father was walking behind him. Abu Hurayrah ran after him and asked, "Who is it who is walking behind you?" I said, "My father." Abu Hurayrah said, "You have made a mistake and contradicted Sunnah. Do not walk in front of your father but walk behind him or on his right and do not let

---

[9] Sunan al-Bayhaqi. But count as not true Hadith by Hadith scholars like Al Albannie .

anyone intercede between you and him. Do not lay hold of a meat steak that your father had laid his eyes on for he might have desired it and do not look sternly at him. Do not sit down until he sits nor sleep until he sleeps."

It was narrated that Abu Hurayrah said that he saw two people, and he said to one of them, "Who is this to you?" He said, "My father." So, he said: "Do not call him by his plain name, nor walk in front of him, nor sit before he sits."

On the authority of Tayla that he said: I said to Ibn Omar, "My mother is with me." So, he said, "Indeed, if you ornamented words for her and offered her food, you would be admitted to the Garden of Paradise as long as you avoided grave sins".

According to Hisham ibn Erwa, according to his father, in reference to the verse: (and spread over them humbly the wings of your tenderness), he said: do not refrain from offering them anything they like.

Al-Hassan was once asked about benevolence towards parents, so he said, "To offer them what you possess and be willing to obey them unless their orders involve sin."

It was narrated that Omar (may Allah be pleased with him) said, "Whoever makes his parents cry is considered undutiful."

BENEVOLENCE TOWARDS PARENTS

On the authority of Salam ibn Mesqeen that he said: I asked Hassan, "Is man allowed to bid his parents what is right and forbid them from what is wrong?" He said: "If they accept; otherwise if they resent, then leave them alone."

Al-Awwam said: I asked Mujahid, "What if the announcer is summoning people for prayer and the messenger of my father is summoning me at the same time?" He said: "Answer your father." Ibn al-Munkadir said: "If your father calls you while you are praying, answer him."

On the authority of Abdul-Samad, he said: I heard Wahab saying, "It is written in the Bible: the top act of benevolence towards parents is to spare them spending their money and feed them from your own."

It was narrated that Abdulah ibn Awn said: "Looking at parents is an act of worship."

• CHAPTER 5 •

The Precedence of The Mother in Benevolence

It was narrated that Abu Hurayrah (may Allah be pleased with him) said: a man asked, "O Messenger of Allah, whoever deserves my good companionship? The Prophet said, "Your mother." The man said, "Then who?" He said, "Your mother." He said, "Then who?' He said, "Your mother." He said, "Then who?" He said, "Your father."[10]

It was narrated that al-Maqdam ibn Ma'ad narrated that the Prophet (peace be upon him) said, "God advises you to take good care of your mothers, God advises you to take good care of your mothers, God advises you to take good care of your mothers, then God recommends that you extend your care to your nearest relatives and kin."[11]

---

[10] Al-Adab Al-Mufrad
[11] Al-Adab Al-Mufrad

On the authority of Khadash bin Abi Salama that he said: the Prophet (peace be upon him) said, "I urge man to take good care of his mother, I urge man to take good care of his mother, I urge man to take good care of his mother, and I urge him to take good care of his father and his servant."[12]

On the authority of al-Awzaa'i, referring to Makuhul that he said: "If your mother calls you while you are praying, answer her. But if your father calls you, do not answer him until you finish."

Anas stated: The Prophet (peace be upon him) said, "The Garden of Paradise lays at the mothers' feet." [13]

It was narrated that Abu Abdul-Rahman al-Salami said: a man came to Abu al-Dard'a and said, "I love my wife, the daughter of Omar, but my mother enjoins me to divorce her." So he said, "I cannot advise you to divorce your wife nor disobey your mother, but I will relate to you a hadith I heard from the Prophet (peace be upon him) saying, "The mother leads you to the middle door of Paradise." So, it's up to you to keep your wife or divorce her." [14]

---

[12] Musnad Ahmad

[13] Ibn Adi the hadith is weak but it the meaning is true and can be found in Sahih Hadith It was narrated from Mu'awiyah bin Jahimah As-Sulami, that Jahimah came to the Prophet (PBUH) and said:
"O Messenger of Allah! I want to go out and fight (in Jihad) and I have come to ask your advice." He said: "Do you have a mother?" He said: "Yes." He said: "Then stay with her, for Paradise is beneath her feet." Sunan an-Nasa'i

BENEVOLENCE TOWARDS PARENTS

Al-Salami narrated that he came to the Prophet (peace be upon him) asking permission for jihad, so the Prophet asked, "Is your mother still living?" The man said, "Yes." The Prophet said, "Keep her company for Paradise is at her feet."[15]

On the authority of Ibn Abbas that the Prophet (peace be upon him) said, "Whoever caresses the eyes of his mother with a kiss is shielded from the Fire."[16]

Anas stated: a man came to the Prophet (peace be upon him) and said, "I long for jihad, but I cannot afford it." The Prophet asked, "Is anyone of your parents still living?" He said, "My mother." The Prophet said, "God has absolved you from jihad in order to show your benevolence towards her. If you did that, it would be as though you have performed complete Hajj and Umrah, and joined jihad, provided she is content with you. So fear God and be benevolent towards her."[17]

It was narrated that Ibn Abbas said that the Prophet (peace be upon him) said, "Whoever looks at his mother with tenderness and compassion is rewarded thereof as though he had performed complete Hajj." The Companions asked, "O Prophet of Allah! Even if we look at her a hundred times a day?" He answered, "Even if you look at her a hundred thousand times a day, God Almighty is more generous and benevolent."[18]

---

[14] Musnad Ahmad
[15] Sunan an-Nasa'i
[16] Ibn Adi the hadith is weak refer to Albani
[17] Hadith Marfoo
[18] Weak Hadith refer to Albani

Ibn Abbas also stated that a man came to him and said, "I proposed to a woman, but she refused to marry me, while someone else proposed to her and she accepted him. I was so jealous that I killed her. Would God accept my repentance?"

Ibn Abbas said: "Is your mother still alive?" He said, "No." He said: "Repent to God and get nearer to Him with works of supererogation as much as you can."

Eventually, someone said to Ibn Abbas, "Why did you ask him whether his mother was alive or not? Ibn Abbas said, "I do not know a deed that brings a Muslim nearer to God than benevolence towards the mother."

It was narrated that Abu Nawfal said: A man came to Omar (may Allah be pleased with him) and said, "I killed a soul." So Omar said, "Woe to you! Willfully or involuntarily?" The man said, "Involuntarily." Omar asked, "Is anyone of your parents still living?". He said, "Yes." Omar asked, "Your mother?" He said, "My father." He said: "Hasten to him and show him your benevolence and kindness." When the man left, Omar said, "Indeed, were his mother still alive and he were benevolent and kind to her, I would have guaranteed that he had guarded himself against the Fire."

Ibn Abbas related: while a man was bringing water from his basin, a thirsty passenger came, so the man said, "Tie the camel and come forward to drink." The passenger descended and tied his camel nearby. When the camel saw the water, it approached the basin which unfortunately collapsed. The owner of the basin

BENEVOLENCE TOWARDS PARENTS

took a sword and killed the passenger. He then wandered about seeking the opinion of the Prophet's Companions, but they thwarted his hopes for a solution to his dilemma until he came to Ibn Abbas. The latter asked him, "Can you revive him just as you killed him?" The man said, "No!" Ibn Abbas asked, "Can you seek a way down into the earth or a ladder unto the sky?" The man said, "No!" Ibn Abbas asked, "Can you live for perpetuity without dying?" When the man intended to walk away, Ibn Abbas said, "Are your parents still alive?" He said, "My mother is." Ibn Abbas said, "Be patient and benevolent to her; perhaps God may guard you against the Fire."

On the authority of al-Hassan that he said, "Allocate your mother two-thirds of your benevolence and allocate your father one-third."

Yaqoub al-Ajli reported: I said to Ata'a, "My mother forbids me to join the congregation prayer on rainy nights." He answered, "Obey your mother."

Ata'a also reported that a mother had sworn that her son should not pray except the obligatory prayers, or fast except the month of Ramadan. He said, "Let him obey her."

Al-Hassan was asked about a man whose father had sworn that he should do something while his mother had sworn a contrary order. He said, "He should obey his mother."

Refaa ibn Iyas said: I saw al-Hares al-Alaki crying at the funeral of his mother, so he was asked, 'Why are you crying?" He said, "How cannot I cry when a door to Paradise has been shut against me?" Refa ibn Iyas again reported: When the mother of Iyas ibn Mu'awiya died, he cried. So, he was asked, "Why are you crying?" He said, "Oh Lord, commend me!" He said, "I commend you to take care of your mother for she has born you going from weakness to weakness." He said, "Then who else?" He said, "Your mother." "Who else?" He said, "Your mother." "Who else?" He said, "Your father."

Hisham ibn Hassan once told al-Hassan, "I learn the Quran while my mother waits for me with dinner all set." Al-Hassan, "In my opinion, to dine with your mother with the intention of pleasing her is better than performing a non-obligatory Hajj."

Al-Hassan ibn Amr narrated that he heard Beshr ibn al-Harith saying, "Any son who stays near his mother within earshot is better than another one striking with his sword for the cause of God and looking at her is better than anything else."

On the authority of Abi Hazim, in reference to Omara who said: I heard my father say, "Woe to you! Didn't you know that looking at your mother is an act of worship, so how about benevolence to her?"

CHAPTER 6

The Reward for Benevolence Towards Parents

It was narrated that Abu Hurayrah heard the Prophet (peace be upon him) saying: "No son can repay his parents' favors unless he finds them slaves, buys them, and sets them free."[19]

The Sheikh stated that it was determined that if a son buys his father, the latter is spontaneously set free under the same deal of purchase, but the son must utter the wording of the emancipation. This is the doctrine of the majority of scholars except Dawood.

The hadith suggests two meanings: the first implies that the father is granted emancipation which spontaneously ensues the purchase deal. The second, which is more precise, suggests that

---

[19] Sahih Muslim

repaying a father's favors is inconceivable, because a son emancipating his father becomes impossible when the purchase deal itself includes his emancipation. In a similar context, God had said, (Nor will they enter the Garden, until the camel can pass through the eye of the needle).

It was narrated that Abdulah ibn Omar said: The Prophet (peace be upon him) said, "Three persons set out on a journey. They were overtaken by rain, so they took shelter in a mountain cave. A big rock fell off the mountain and rested at the mouth of the cave, blocking any way for exit. One of them said to the others: Summon to your minds your good deeds that you performed for the sake of God and invoke Him in reference to them that He might relieve you from your difficulty. One of them said: O God, I was living with my old parents, my wife and my small children. I used to tend to the grazing of the sheep and afterwards milk them. I used to offer milk to my parents first. One day I came home late to find my parents asleep. I cleared the bowl, milked the animals, and stood with the bowl of milk by their heads. My children, starving as they were, kept weeping at my feet. I did not deem it right to offer milk to my children before my parents and, at the same time, hated to disturb their sleep. I remained there in that very state until the crack of dawn. O God, if You know that I did this only for Your sake, then make a gap from which we can see the sky. The rock slipped a bit and they could see the sky. And he mentioned the rest of the hadith.[20]

BENEVOLENCE TOWARDS PARENTS

It was narrated that Aysha (may Allah be pleased with her) said: The Prophet (peace be upon him) said, "I had a nap and found myself in Paradise. Then I heard someone reciting so I said, "Who is this?" They said, "Haritha ibn an-Nu'man." The Prophet said: "Indeed, benevolence pays off; he was most benevolent towards his mother."[21]

Makhoul stated: the delegation of the al-Ash'aryeen came to the Prophet (peace be upon him) and he asked them, "Is Wajera among you?" They said, "Yes!" The Prophet said, "God has admitted her to Paradise due to her benevolence towards her mother who was a pagan. Her neighborhood was invaded, so she carried her mother and dashed out into the sweltering desert. When her feet burned from heat, she used to sit, seat her mother in her lap, and shade her from the sun. When rest was over, she resumed her course while carrying her."[22]

Abdul-Rahman ibn Samra reported: The Prophet (peace be upon him) came one day while we were in the mosque of Medina and said, "I saw a man from my community whom the Angel of death came to take his soul but his benevolence towards his parents interceded and sent the Angel back."[23]

---

[20] Sahih al-Bukhari
[21] Musnad Ahmad
[22] Couldn't Find the source
[23] Al Hethamie weak Hadith

Abu ad-Dardaa reported: Omar (may Allah be pleased with him) said, "We were with the Prophet (peace be upon him) over a mountain when we came to see a valley. I beheld a young man and I admired his youth, so I said: 'O Prophet of Allah, were his youth invested for the sake of God?' The Prophet (peace be upon him) said: 'O Omar, perhaps it is for the sake of God, but you do not know.' When the young man approached, the Prophet asked him, 'O young man, is there anyone depending on you for his livelihood?' He said, 'Yes.' He said, 'Who?' He said, 'My mother.' The Prophet said, 'Keep near her for Paradise is at her feet.'"[24]

Mowarik al-Ujali also narrated: The Prophet (peace be upon him) said, "Do you know of any spending better than spending for the cause of God?" They said, "God and His Messenger know best." He said, "A son's spending on his parents is better."[25]

---

[24] Jama Al Hadith
[25] Couldn't find the source

• CHAPTER 7 •

Ultimate Benevolence Towards Parents

It was narrated that Aysha (may Allah be pleased with her) said: Two of the Companions of the Prophet (peace be upon him) were most benevolent towards their mothers; Othman ibn Affan, and Haritha ibn an-Nu'man (may Allah be pleased with them both). As for Othman, he said, "I could not look at my mother straight in the face since I embraced Islam."

While Haritha used to comb his mother's hair to remove lice and feed her with his hand. Whenever her orders were incomprehensible to him, he never inquired about it until she went out, then he asked whoever was present, "What did my mother want?"

Abu Hurayrah narrated that whenever he wanted to leave his house, he would stand at his mother's door and say, "Peace, mercy and blessings of Allah be upon you, mother." She would say, "Peace, mercy and blessings of Allah be upon you, my son." He would then say, "May God bestow His mercy on you, just as you reared and nurtured me when I was a child." She would reply, "May God bestow His mercy on you, just as you were benevolent to me when you became a man."

Whenever he entered the house, he acted in the same manner.

Abu Umamah narrated that Abu Hurayrah (may Allah be pleased with him) used to carry his mother to the rest room and lift her off, and she was blind."

Ibn Sirin said, "The price of the palm-tree reached thousand dirhams. So, when I made a hole in a palm-tree to get palm pith, they told me, 'You made a hole in a palm tree that costs a fortune to obtain palm pith that costs two dirhams?'" So, I said, 'My mother asked me for it, and if she had asked me for something more than that, I would have obeyed.'"

It was narrated that Sufian al-Thawri said: Ibn al-Hanafiyah used to wash his mother's hair with hibiscus, comb it, and grease it.

Az-Zuhari said: al-Hassan ibn Ali used to abstain from eating with his mother, although he was most benevolent to her. So, he was asked about the reason for this. He said, "I fear lest she should lay her eye on certain food while I am unaware; so when I eat it, I would become undutiful to her."

In another narration, "I fear lest my hand precedes hers."

BENEVOLENCE TOWARDS PARENTS

On the authority of Ismail bin Awn that he reported: a man visited Ibn Sirin while his mother was with him. So, he said: "Is Muhammad sick?" They told him, "No! But this is the case when he is with his mother."

Hisham stated: Hafsah used to commemorate Hozail and ask God to rest his soul. She said, "He used to peel the canes and dry them in summer, so it would not produce any smoke. When winter came, he used to sit behind me while I was praying and set up a gentle fire that would warm me up without producing irritating smoke. I often told him, "My son, go back to your family tonight." And he says, "O, mother, I know what they want." So, I leave him alone and he may remain like this till morning.

He also used to send me milk that was produced in the morning and I say, 'My son, you know that I do not drink during day,' and he replies, 'The best milk is what stays in the udder all night and I don't want to give precedence to anyone on you. You can send it to whomever you like.'

Then Hozail died and I cried my heart out grieving on him. My chest was burning with inconsolable melancholy. She said: One night, I stayed up praying and started reciting surat an-Nahl until I came to the verse: (That which is with you will come to an end, but that which is with God remains. And He shall surely pay those who were patient, their reward according to the best of what they used to do). Only then did I find rest and reassurance."

Anas ibn an-Nadr al-Ashja'i related: one night, Ibn Mas'ud's mother wanted some water. So, he went and came back with it, only to find her asleep. So, he waited with the drink at her head until morning.

Similarly, Zubayn ibn Ali al-Thawri, who was most benevolent towards his mother, said, "One night, my mother slept angry with me, so I kept standing on my feet, reluctant to wake her up or sit down. When my legs failed under me, two of my boys came and supported me until she woke up."

He used to take her to Mecca, and when it was hot, he would dig a hole in the ground, lay a leather mat, and pour water on it. He would then bid her, "Get into the water and cool yourself."

Muhammad ibn Omar also narrated: Muhammad ibn Abdul-Rahman ibn Abi az-Zanad was benevolent towards his mother. When his father calls him, "O Muhammad!" He would not answer him until he approached him and asked him his need. If the father's order was incomprehensible, he would not ask for clarification out of reverence for him. Instead, he would ask someone else who was able to understand better.

When Awn ibn Abdullah's mother called out for him and he answered in a loud voice, he emancipated two slaves.

BENEVOLENCE TOWARDS PARENTS

On the authority of Bakr ibn Abbas that he said: perhaps I was sitting with Mansour when his mother shouted, and she was harsh and violent, saying: "O Mansoor! Ibn Habira wants to appoint you on top of the Judiciary and you refuse?" And he would keep his beard on his chest without even raising his eyes.

Sayfan ibn Oyynah said: a man came back from travelling while his mother was standing performing her prayers. He did not deem it right to sit while his mother was standing. When she realized what he wanted, she prolonged her prayer so that he would be better rewarded for his dutifulness.

When Omar ibn Tharr's son died, people inquired about his benevolence. He said, "When I walked by day, he used to walk behind me and when I walked by night, he used to walk in front of me. He never lay on a roof while I was under it."

Al-Ma'ali ibn Awb recounted: I heard al-Ma'mun saying, "No one was more benevolent towards his father than al-Fadl ibn Yahya al-Baramqi. The former used to perform his ablution with warm water. One cold night, when they were in prison together, the warden did not permit letting some firewood in. When the father was asleep, al-Fadl took a flask, filled it with water and placed it near the lamp. He kept standing with the flask in his hand until morning.

Another narration, not related by al-Ma'mun, said that when the warden noticed that al-Fadl used the lamp to heat the water, he held back the lamp the following night. So, al-Fadl took the flask which was full of water with him to bed and held it tightly to his chest until morning, so the water warmed up.

Ka'ab al-Ahbar related: Three men from the Children of Israel gathered one day and said, "Let everyone of us mention the most grievous offence he has ever committed."

So, one of them said: "I do not remember a greater offence than when urine soiled our garments, we used to cut off the part that was soiled, but when my garment was soiled with urine, I did not cut too much cloth. This is the gravest offence I have ever done."

The other said, "I was with my companion when a tree interceded between us. When I came out from around the tree, he was startled and said: God is the judge between us."

The third said, "One day, when my mother called me, but the wind hindered her hearing my answer. Vexed as she was, she came to me and started to throw me with stones. So, I took a stick and came to sit in front of her, so she can strike me with it. She was frightened that she hit a tree and cut her face. This is the greatest offence I have contrived."

• CHAPTER 8 •

The Sin of Being Undutiful Towards Parents

Abu Bakra quoted, according to his father: When the major sins were mentioned in the presence of the Prophet (peace be upon him), he said, "Associating partners with God, being undutiful towards parents," then he sat upright after he was leaning and said, "And perjury". He kept repeating it until we said, "If only he would be silent."[26]

Anas quoted the Prophet (peace be upon him) saying when asked about the major sins, "Associating partners with God, killing a human being, being undutiful to parents, ..) and he mentioned the rest of the hadith.[27]

Ibn Omar narrated that the Prophet (peace be upon him) said, "The most grievous sins are: associating partners with God,

---

[26] Sahih by Imam albani
[27] Muslim

being undutiful towards parents, killing a human being, and perjury."[28]

The Prophet was quoted saying, "He will never be admitted to Paradise who is undutiful towards his parents, addicted to liquors, disbelieves in destiny, or lies under oath."[29]

Ibn Omar reported that the Prophet (peace be upon him) said, "God will not look at three types of people on the Day of Resurrection: a man who is undutiful to his parents; a man who is addicted to liquors, a man who is boastful of what he has given in charity."[30]

Abu Hurayrah quoted that the Prophet (peace be upon him) said, "Four types of people God will never permit to be admitted to Paradise or enjoy its pleasure: one who is addicted to alcoholics, one who consumes usury, one who devours an orphan's property, and one who is undutiful to his parents."[31]

On the authority of Zayd ibn Arqam that he said: I heard the Prophet saying, "Whoever is endowed with the satisfaction of his parents every morning, will have two open doors to the Garden of Paradise. Whoever is endowed with the satisfaction of his parents every evening, will have two open doors to the Garden of Paradise. Whereas, whoever incurs the dissatisfaction

---

[28] Al Bukhari
[29] Al Albani
[30] Ibn Hiban
[31] Al Hakim

of his parents every morning, will have two open doors to the Fire; if it is only one of his parents, then there will be one door. So, someone said, "Even if they were unjust to him?" He said, "Even if they were unjust to him, even if they were unjust to him, even if they were unjust to him." [32]

Amr ibn Murrah al-Johani related: a man came to the Prophet (peace be upon him) and said, "O Messenger of Allah, I bear witness that there is no god but God, and that you are the Messenger of God; I will observe the five prayers, pay the Zakat (obligatory alms), and fast the month of Ramadan." The Prophet said, "Whoever did this and died will be with the prophets, the truthful, the martyrs, and the righteous on the Day of Judgment as such - and he stuck his two fingers together - unless he is undutiful to his parents."[33]

Abu Hurayrah narrated that the Prophet (peace be upon him) ascended the pulpit and said, "Amen, Amen, Amen."

When he descended, he was asked, "O Messenger of Allah, when you stepped up the pulpit, you said: Amen three times!" He said, "Jibril (Gabriel) came to me and said:

Whoever failed to be forgiven in Ramadan, so he died and was cast into the Fire, let God seclude him away. He bid me say Amen, so I said: Amen. Whoever caught up with his parents or one of them in their old age, but was undutiful to them, so he

---

[32] Al Dar Qutnie
[33] Ibn khuzimah

died and was cast into the Fire, let God seclude him away. He bid me say Amen, so I said: Amen. Whoever hears you mentioned in his presence and did not invoke blessings on you, so he died and was cast into the Fire, let God seclude him away. He bid me say Amen, so I said: Amen."[34]

On the authority of Abi Tofayl that he said: Ali (may Allah be pleased with him) was asked: Did the Prophet (peace be upon him) assign you anything in particular that he did not assign to the rest of the people? He said, "The Prophet did not assign anything to us that he did not assign to the rest of the people except what is in the sheath of my sword." He brought out a scroll in which was written (God has cursed whoever offered a sacrifice which was not in His name. God has cursed whoever stole the guiding light of land. God has cursed whoever was undutiful to his parents).[35]

Abu Hurayrah quoted: The Prophet (peace be upon him) said, "May he be disgraced! May he be disgraced!" They asked, "Who do you mean, O Messenger of Allah?" He said, "Who caught up with his parents, or one of them, in their old age and was not admitted to the Garden of Paradise." [36]

---

[34] Abu yeala
[35] Musnad Ahmad
[36] There is a similar hadith with same meaning in Sahih Muslim" Abu Huraira reported Allah's Messenger (PBUH) as saying:
Let him be humbled, let him be humbled. It was said: Allah's Messenger, who is he? He said. He who finds his parents in old age, either one or both of them, and does not enter Paradise.

BENEVOLENCE TOWARDS PARENTS

Ibn 'Abbaas (may Allah be pleased with him) reported that the Prophet (peace be upon him) said, "Cursed is he who curses his father. Cursed is he who curses his father."[37]

It was narrated that Abu Hurayrah (may Allah be pleased with him) heard the Prophet (peace be upon him) saying, "Of all His creation, God has cursed seven types of people from over the seven heavens: Cursed is he whoever was undutiful to his parents..."(the hadith). [38] He also related that the Prophet said: "God does not accept the prayer of whoever incurs the displeasure of his parents provided they are just to him."[39]

Anas heard the Messenger of Allah (peace be upon him) saying, "Whoever earns his parents' satisfaction, will similarly earn God's satisfaction. Whoever incurs his parents' displeasure, will similarly incur God's displeasure."[40]

According to Aysha (may Allah be pleased with her), the Prophet (peace be upon him) said, "God says to the undutiful towards his parents: Do whatever you want, I won't forgive you. And says to the dutiful towards his parents: Do whatever you want, I will forgive you."[41]

---

[37] Musnad Ahmad
[38] AL Bahaeqi
[39] Abu Al Hassan bin Maroouf
[40] Jama Al Ahadeth
[41] Couldn't find the source

It was narrated that Abu Bakra said that the Prophet (peace be upon him) said, "Any sin can wait to be requited in the Day of the Resurrection except undutifulness to parents; it is requited in this life).[42]

Anas (may Allah be pleased with him) quoted the Prophet (peace be upon him) said, "God has revealed to Moses, the son of Imran (peace be upon him): O Moses, a word uttered by an undutiful son to his parents is indeed most heinous to me. They said: 'O Moses, what is this word?' He said: "to tell his parents: Go away and leave me alone."[43]

Some wise man said, "Do not befriend the undutiful to his parents: how could he be kind to you when he was unkind to those who had more claim to him?"

---

[42] Al Mustdrak
[43] Couldn't find the source

• CHAPTER 9 •

The ill-fate of the undutiful

It was narrated that Abdulah ibn' Ufay said: A man came to the Prophet (peace be upon him) and said: "O Messenger of Allah, a lad is now on his deathbed but cannot utter the testimony to the Oneness of God. The Prophet asked, "Didn't he it say in his life?" They said, "Yes". So, he said, "Then what prevents him from saying it when he is dying?" The Prophet and his Companions went to see the boy. He bade him say, "There is no god but God." The lad said, "I can't say it." The Prophet said, "Why not?" The boy said, "Because I was disobedient to my mother". He asked: "Is she alive?" He said, "Yes." So, they summoned her. The Prophet said, "This is your son?" She said, "Yes." He said, "You see, if a big fire was set up and you were told: if you did not intercede on behalf of your son, we will bury him right in this fire." She said, "Definitely I would intercede." He said: "So bear witness to God and to us that you are satisfied with him." She said, "O God, I bear witness to You and to your Messenger that I am satisfied with my son. The Prophet said, "O lad, say: There is no god but God." He said, "There is no god but God." The Prophet (peace upon him) said, "Praise be to God who saved him, through my intervention, from the Fire."[44]

Malik ibn Dinar narrated: While I was doing the tawaf round the Sacred House, I admired the multitude of pilgrims and said, "If only I could know whose pilgrimage was accepted so I would congratulate him, and whose pilgrimage was rejected so I would offer him my condolences."

That night, I saw in my dreams someone saying, "Malik ibn Dinar is asking about the pilgrims? God has forgiven them all, the young and the old, the male and the female, the black and the red, except for one man who has incurred God's wrath so He has rejected his pilgrimage.

Malik said, "God only knows how I spent that night lest I should be that man. On the second night, I saw the same vision but I was told that I was not that man. He is from Khurasan from the city of Balakh and he is called, Muhammad ibn Harun al-Bolakhi.

In the morning, I went to the tribes of Khurasan and asked, "Where is your brother Muhammad ibn Harun?" They said, "You are asking about a man who is unparalleled in Khurasan in his worship, abstention, and recitation of Quran."

---

[44] AL Aqalei , False Hadith by Al bani

BENEVOLENCE TOWARDS PARENTS

I was perplexed by the people's high opinion and praise for him and what I saw in my vision. So, I said, "Lead me to him." They said, "For forty years, he had been fasting

by day, praying by night, and residing in ruins. He might be in some ruins of Mecca."

I wandered for some time among the ruins till I found him standing behind a wall, and his right hand attached to his neck and bound with chains to his feet, kneeling and prostrating. When he felt my presence, he said, "Who are you?" I said, "Malik ibn Dinar." He said, "O Malik! Why did you come to me? If you have seen a vision, relate it to me." He said, "I am too ashamed to relate it." He said, "Go ahead; say it." So, I related my vision to him and he cried for a long time, and said, "I was a man addicted to drink and one day I got very drunk and was out of my mind. When I got home, I found my mother igniting the furnace. When she saw me staggering, she approached to give me food, saying: This is the last day of the month of Sha'baan and the first night of Ramadan; people will wake up fasting while you wake up drunk! Aren't you ashamed of yourself in front of God? I lifted my hand and nudged her. So she said, "Woe to you!" I became so angry that I carried her, being excessively drunk, and threw her into the burning furnace. When my wife saw this, she locked me up in some house.

Late that night, when I began to regain my consciousness, I asked my wife to open the door but she answered me sternly. So I inquired why she was being so stern and she said, "You don't deserve compassion." I asked, "Why?" She said, "You killed your mother. You cast her into the furnace and she got burnt."

So I rushed to the furnace to find her like a burnt loaf of bread. I donated my money in charity and emancipated my slaves. For forty years now, I have been fasting by day, praying by night, and performing Hajj every year, and every year, a worshipper like you envisions me in his dream.

I jabbed him in the face and said, "O ill-fated man, you almost burned the earth with what thereupon with your fire." Then I walked away so that I could hear him without being able to see him. He raised his hands to the sky, and said, 'O Reliever of distress, Remover of sorrow, who answers the desperate. I seek refuge in Your pleasure from Your wrath, and in Your forgiveness from Your punishment, do not thwart my hope or reject my supplication."

So, I went home and slept. I saw in my dream someone saying, "O Malik, do not thwart people's aspiration to God's mercy. God has looked upon Muhammad ibn Harun from above and accepted his supplication and relieved his distress. Go back to him and tell him, "God gathers all the creatures on the Day of the Resurrection so that the hornless sheep would get its claim from the horned. And you will be reunited with your mother and God will judge for her against you. You will taste the Fire and then He will deliver you to your mother.".

CHAPTER 10

Aspects of being undutiful

It was narrated that Abdulah ibn Omar (may Allah be pleased with them both) said, "Inducing the parents to cry is disobedience."

Omar ibn az-Zubayr said, "Whoever looks sternly at his parents has committed an act of disobedience."

Muhammad ibn Sirin quoted, "Whoever walks in front of his father has lost his mind, except for removing the harm from his way. And whoever calls his father with his plain name has lost his mind except for addressing him with: O Father."

On the authority of Mujahid that he said, "A son ought not to push away his father's hand if he strikes him. Whoever looks sternly at his parents is not benevolent towards them. And whoever causes their grief is undutiful."

Al-Hassan al-Basri stated, "It is absolute estrangement for a man to disoblige his father in the presence of the sovereign."

Farqad said: I read in some books: "Whoever cast a sharp look at his parents is undutiful, whereas looking at them is an act of worship. A son should not walk in front of his father or speak in his presence. He should not walk on their right or on their left unless they call him, so he answers them, or order him so he obeys them; he should walk behind them like a humble slave."

Yazid ibn Abi Habib said: "Invalidating the argument of the parents is disobedience." i.e. to refute their argument.

Ka'ab al-Ahbar was asked about disobedience, so he said: "It is absolute disobedience when your parents command you with something and you disobey."

Acceptance of the parents' supplication for the son

Abdulah ibn Mas'ud said, "Three supplications are never rejected: that of the father, the oppressed, and the traveler."

Al-Hassan said, "The blessing of the parents' supplication yields wealth and children."

Al-Hassan was asked: What is a father's supplication to his son? He said, "Rescue."

Mujahid narrated, "Three supplications are not concealed from God Almighty: the supplication of the oppressed, the supplication of the father for his son, and the testimony to the Oneness of God."

He also said, "The supplication of the father is not hidden from God Almighty."

BENEVOLENCE TOWARDS PARENTS

It was narrated that Abdul-Rahman ibn Ahmad ibn Hanbal said: I heard my father say, "A woman came to Mukhalad ibn al-Hussayn and said, "My son was taken captive by the Romans and I cannot afford to pay his ransom. If only you could guide me to someone who can pay it for I cannot sleep or rest night or day."

The Sheikh sat thinking and said some prayers and invocations. Then, some time elapsed and the woman came with her son and kept invoking blessings for him and said, "The young man will relate his story." He said, "I was taken captive by some Roman kings with other prisoners. While we were returning from work after sunset, the chains tied to my feet opened and fell to the ground."

He assigned the day and the hour which coincided with the time when his mother came to the Sheikh and they both prayed for him.

"My guard shouted at me, "You have broken the chains!" I said, "No, they fell off." The guard was astonished and informed his companion who brought the blacksmith and chained me. I had barely walked a few steps when the chains fell off again. They were bewildered and summoned their monks who asked me, "Do you have a mother?"

I said, "Yes." They said: "Her supplication has been accepted; God has released you so we cannot chain you. They gave me supplies and accompanied me towards the Muslims' land."

Ibn Qayyim Al-Jawziyya

Acceptance of the parents' imprecation on the son

It was narrated that Abu Hurayrah (may Allah be pleased with him) said that the Prophet (peace be upon him) said, "Three supplications are directly accepted: that of the oppressed, that of the traveler, and that of parents imprecating on their son."[45]

He also narrated that the Prophet (peace be upon him) said, "Goraig was a monk living in a hermitage and there was a shepherd residing under the hermitage. A villager woman used to visit the shepherd. One day, Goraig's mother called him, "O Goraig," while he was praying. He hesitated between answering his mother and continuing his prayer but he decided to give precedence to his prayer. She called aloud for a second and a third time, but he did not answer. So, she said, "May you never die until you look at the faces of the prostitutes," and left.

Then the woman gave birth to a child. When they asked her, "Who is the child's father?" She said, "Goraig." So, they destroyed his hermitage, tied chains to his neck, and dragged him along passing on their way by the prostitutes. He smiled when they looked at him.

He asked the king, "What does this woman claim?" He said, "She claims that the child is yours."

So, he approached the baby and said, "Who is your father?" The baby said, "The shepherd." The king, out of astonishment,

---

[45] Musnad Ahmad

said, "We will build you a hermitage of gold!" He said, "No, rebuild it the same way it was." The king asked, "Why were you smiling then?" He said, "I was stricken with my mother's imprecation," and he related the story.[46]

Disowning parents or children

On the authority of Anas al-Johani, referring to his father that the Prophet (peace be upon him) said, "Some people God shall not speak to them, nor look upon them on the Day of Resurrection, nor will He purify them." He was asked, "Who are those, O Messenger of Allah?" He said, "A disowner of his parents who turns away from them; a disowner of his son and a man who was endowed with the favors of some people but he denied these favors and renounced them."[47]

Abu Hurayrah (may Allah be pleased with him) reported that the Prophet (peace be upon him) said, "Whoever disowns his child while he looks upon him (realizing that he is actually his son), God will forsake him, and scandalize him in public for all the people to see."[48]

The sin of designating a child to someone other than his father

---

[46] Al Adab Al Mufrad
[47] Musnad Ahmad
[48] sunan abi dawud

On the authority of Ibrahim al-Tamimi, in reference to his father, that he said: Ali (may Allah be pleased with him) delivered a sermon and said, "Whoever claims that we have any other references to read than the Quran and this scroll - a scroll in which the teeth of camels and rulings of surgeries – has lied. The Messenger of Allah (peace be upon him) said in it, "Cursed is he whoever claimed a father other than his own or managed slaves other than his own; cursed by God and the angels and all the people, and God will not accept compensation or intercession on his behalf."[49]

Ibn 'Uthmaan al-Hindi stated: I heard Sa'ad saying: I heard with my ears and comprehended with my heart the Prophet (peace be upon him) saying, "(Whoever claims a father other than his own, will be forbidden from admittance to Paradise."

He said: I then met Abu Bakr and related to him the hadith and he said, "I heard it too from the Messenger of Allah peace be upon him."[50]

It was narrated that Abu Zara'a said that the Prophet (peace be upon him) said, "Do not renounce your fathers. Whoever renounces his father has renounced religion."

---

[49] sunan al tirmidhi
[50] In Muslim with different Narration

BENEVOLENCE TOWARDS PARENTS

The punishment of causing the parents to be cursed

It was narrated that Abdulah ibn Omar said that the Messenger of Allah (peace be upon him) said, "One of the gravest sins is when man curses his parents." He was asked, "How on earth would a man curse his parents?" He said, "He would curse someone's father, so the latter would curse his father and his mother."[51]

The permissibility for father to claim back his gift

Ibn Abbas reported that Prophet (peace be upon him) said, "It is not permissible for a man who believes in God and the Day of Judgment to claim back his gift except for the father."

In a similar context, Ibn Omar and Ibn Abbas quoted that the Prophet (peace be upon him) said, "It is not permissible for a man to claim back his gift, except for what the father has given his son.".[52]

.

---

[51] Al-Bukhari & Muslim
[52] Sunnan Abi Dawuid

• CHAPTER 11 •

Connecting with Parents After Their Death

Abu Hurayrah (may Allah be pleased with him) narrated that the Prophet (peace be upon him) said, "When a man dies, his actions cease to exist except for three things, namely, perpetual charity, the knowledge by which benefit is acquired, and a pious child who prays for him."[53]

It was narrated that Anas ibn Malik (may Allah be pleased with him) said that the Prophet (peace be upon him) said: "Man is rewarded in his life as well as after his death for seven deeds: whoever imparts knowledge onto others, lets a river flow, digs a well, plants a palm-tree, builds a mosque, bequeaths Quran, or leaves behind a son asking forgiveness for him."[54]

---

[53] Muslim
[54] Al Bazar, Sahih by Imam Albani

As-Saddey ibn Obayd, according to his father, said: A man asked, "O Messenger of Allah, is there any act of dutifulness which I can still offer my parents after they die?" He answered, "Yes. You can do four things: supplication for them, asking forgiveness for them, fulfilling their pledges, being generous to their friends, and fostering ties of their kinship."[55]

Abu Hurayrah reported that the Prophet (peace be upon him) said, "God will raise the status of a good man in Paradise and he will say: 'O God, where did this come from?' He will say, "Through your son's praying for forgiveness for you."[56]

It was narrated that Mu'adh ibn Jabal said that the Messenger of Allaah (peace be upon him) said: " Whoever recites the Qur'an and acts according to its rulings, his parents will be given a crown to wear on the Day of Resurrection whose light is better than the light of the sun in the dwellings of this world. So what do you think of him who acts according to this?"[57]

On the authority of Abi Kahil that the Prophet (peace be upon him) said, "Whoever was dutiful to his parents in their life and after their death is apt to be granted what satisfies him on the Day of Resurrection." So we said, "How will he be dutiful to them when they are dead?" He said, "Through asking

---

[55] Sunan Abi Dawuid
[56] Musnad Ahmad
[57] Sunan Abi Dawuid

BENEVOLENCE TOWARDS PARENTS

forgiveness for them and abstaining from cursing anyone's parents so that his parents would not subsequently be cursed."

Ibn Abbas narrated that the Prophet (peace be upon him) said, "The gift of the living to the dead is to ask forgiveness for them. God will admit whatever the people still residing in this world offer those residing in the graves even if they were as huge as mountains."[58]

Amr ibn Shu'aib, according to his father, according to his grandfather, that the Prophet (peace be upon him) said, "It is better for someone donating charity to donate it in the name of his parents provided they are Muslims, so his parents will have their reward without deducting anything from his own reward."[59]

Ibn Abbas narrated that Sa'ad ibn Obadah's mother died while he was away. So he said, "O Messenger of Allah, my mother died while I was away. Would it avail her if I donate charity on her behalf?" He said, "Yes." Sa'ad said, "I bear you witness that I give this garden of mine in charity on her behalf."[60]

Abu Hurayrah stated that a man said to the Prophet (peace be upon him): "O Messenger of Allah, my mother died. Would it avail her if I donate charity on her behalf?" He said, "Yes."

On the authority of Ibn Abbas that the Prophet (peace be upon him) said, "Whoever performs Hajj on behalf of his

---

[58] AL modawat Ibn Al Jawzei
[59] Couldn't find the source
[60] Al Bukhari

parents or pays their debts will be resurrected with the righteous."[61]

Fostering the ties of their kinship and friendship

Ibn Omar narrated that a nomad dropped by his house while he was traveling, and he was a friend of Omar's. The nomad said, "Aren't your so-and-so, the son of so-and-so?" He said, "Yes." Ibn Omar, then, provided him with a donkey to exchange it with his riding animal when one of them needed rest, and removed the turban from his head and gave it to him. So someone said, "It was enough if you have given him a dirham." Ibn Omar said, "The Prophet (peace upon him) said "Observe and foster the affection towards your father's friends. Don't sever it or God will extinguish your light."[62]

It was narrated that Nafi' said: Abu Burda arrived at Medina, so Ibn Omar (may Allah be pleased with him) came to visit and greet him. When he wanted to leave, he said, "I heard the Messenger of Allah (peace be upon him) say, "One of the best acts of benevolence towards parents is to foster the connection with the friends of one's father after his death." And my father was a friend of your father's, so I paid you this visit to foster the ties of my father's friendship."[63]

---

[61] Sunan Dar Qutni
[62] Al Adab Al Mufrad
[63] Muslim, narrated with different chain

BENEVOLENCE TOWARDS PARENTS

Omar ibn al-Khattab (may Allah be pleased with him) said: "Whoever wants to be benevolent towards his father in his grave, let him foster the ties between him and his father's brothers after his death."

Visiting their grave

It was narrated that Abu Hurayrah said: the Prophet (peace be upon him) visited his mother's grave and wept, so all those who were present wept too. Then he said, "I asked God Almighty to visit their grave, so He permitted me, and I asked Him to beg forgiveness for them but He did not grant me permission."[64]

Aysha (may Allah be pleased with her), according to her father, that he heard the Prophet (peace be upon him) say: "Whoever visits the grave of his parents or one of them on Friday and recites Yassin (a chapter in the Quran) will be forgiven."[65]

Abdulah ibn Omar stated that the Prophet (peace be upon him) said, "Whoever visits his mother's grave, or the grave of one of his relatives, will be rewarded as though he had performed complete hajj. And whoever keeps visiting their graves until he dies, the angels will visit his grave."[66]

---

[64] Muslim
[65] Al Tabrani, not True Hadith as per Imam Albani
[66] Al Tabrani, not True Hadith as per Imam Albani

Othman ibn Saudah's mother was a fervent worshiper whom they called: the nun. He said, "When she was dying, she raised her head to the sky and said, "O My Sustainer and Maintainer at my death, do not leave me lonely and desolate in my grave."

He said, "Then she died, and I used to visit her grave every Friday to pray for her and ask forgiveness for her and for the other people in the graves. One night, I saw her in my sleep, and I said, "O mother, how are you?" She said, "O my son, death involves great distress, but I am, thank God, in an admirable Barrier, sprawling basil underneath us and leaning on the finest silk and gold embroidery till the Day of Resurrection."

I said, "Do you need anything?" She said, "Yes, don't stop visiting us and praying for us for I rejoice at your visit every Friday. When you come, they call me: O nun, here is your son leaving his family to pay you a visit. So, I rejoice as well as the others around me from among the dead."

Praised is he who said,

Visit your parents' grave and wait at it ...   for if you were now in their position

And they were still alive ....   they would have come to you on their knees crawling

They have sheltered you with their religion ...   and protected you with their affection

Should they notice a sign of ailment in you ...bitter grief will start to gnaw at their bosom

BENEVOLENCE TOWARDS PARENTS

If they hear you whining ... they would cry their eyes out in compassion

And wishing that all ways for relieving you ... were at their disposition

Soon you will join them ... just as they joined their parents in succession

So, give precedence to their affairs ...just as they gave their parents out of benefaction

Blessed are you offering benevolence ... and repaying them some of your obligation

And staying at night asking for forgiveness... and prolonging your prayers in their commemoration

And reciting verses of the Quran intending ... to send them their reward in the world beyond

And donate charity from your money ... just as they assigned their parents their donation

Observe my advice for you and try to apply it...for you will be the winner when you show your benefaction

Al-Fadl ibn Mawqaf reported, "I used to pay frequent visits to my father's grave. One day, I attended a funeral, and when the dead man was buried, I hastened back to make an errand and did not visit my father's grave. I saw him in my sleep and he said, "My son, why did not you come?" I said, "O father, you know that I come?" He said, "Yes, I swear to God I do; I keep looking at you when you cross the vault and sit by my side until you leave, and I keep looking at you until you cross the vault and walk away."

• CHAPTER 12 •

The Reward of Fostering Ties Of Kinship And The Punishment For Severing It

Anas (may Allah be pleased with him) related that the Prophet (peace be upon him) said, "Whoever wishes to attain blessings in his life and his livelihood, let him fear God and foster the ties of his kinship."[67]

It was narrated that Ali (may Allah be pleased with him) said that the Prophet (peace be upon him) said, "Whoever wishes to attain blessings in his life and his livelihood, and avoid ill-fated death, let him fear God and foster the ties of his kinship."[68]

---

[67] Muslim & Bukhari
[68] Al Hakim

Aysha (may Allah be pleased with her) quoted that the Prophet (peace be upon him) said, "Fostering ties of kinship and good neighborliness make homes prosperous and lives lengthy."[69]

On the authority of Abu Umamah (may Allah be pleased with him) said that the Prophet (peace be upon him) said, "Acts of benevolence prevent ill-fated deaths, while charity in secret quenches God's wrath, and fostering the ties of kinship makes lives lengthy."[70]

Abu Sa'eed al-Khudri stated that the Prophet (peace be upon him) said, "The owners of these five attributes will not be admitted to the Garden of Paradise: being addicted to liquors, believing in magic, severing one's ties of kinship, soothsaying, and being boastful of one's charity."[71]

Abu Hurayrah (may Allah be pleased with him) said that the Prophet (peace be upon him) said, "The deeds of all human beings are revealed to God every Thursday – Friday night, but He will not accept the deeds of someone severing the ties of his kinship."[72]

Abu Hurayrah quoted that the Prophet (peace be upon him) said, "When God concluded His creation, ties of kinship came

---

[69] Sahih by Albani
[70] Al Buhaeqi
[71] Musnad Ahmad
[72] Musnad Ahmad

BENEVOLENCE TOWARDS PARENTS

forth and said, "O Allah, at this place I seek refuge in You against severing my ties." Allah said: 'Will you be satisfied if I foster ties with those who foster yours and sever ties with those who sever yours! Recite if you want, [73]

فَهَلْ عَسَيْتُمْ إِن تَوَلَّيْتُمْ أَن تُفْسِدُوا فِي الْأَرْضِ وَتُقَطِّعُوا أَرْحَامَكُمْ (22)

(Would you then, if you were given the authority, do mischief in the land, and sever your ties of kinship? Such are they whom Allah has cursed, so that He has deafened them and blinded their sight.) [74]

Aysha (may Allah be pleased with her) related that the Prophet (peace be upon him) said, "The ties of kinship are hanging by the throne of God saying, whoever fosters my ties of kinship, God will foster His ties with him, and whoever severs the ties of my kinship, God will sever His ties with him."[75]

On the authority of Abu Bakra that the Prophet (peace be upon him) said, "No sin is apt to hasten God's punishment in this world, with what awaits him in the Afterlife, worse than severing the ties of one's kinship and oppression."[76]

---

[73] Muslim
[74] Quran 47:22
[75] Muslim
[76] Sunan Abi Dawud

Ibn Qayyim Al-Jawziyya

Abu Awfa said, "Mercy does not descend upon a group of people among whom there is someone severing the ties of his kinship."

Abu Hurayrah (may Allah be pleased with him) narrated that he said: I said, "O Messenger of Allah, when I see you, I become delighted and tranquil. Inform me about everything." He said, "Everything is created from water."
I said, "Guide me to a deed that admits me to the Garden of Paradise." He said, "Feed one another, spread peace, foster ties of kinship, pray at night while others are asleep - then you shall enter the Garden of Paradise in peace."[77]

On the authority of Anas (may Allah be pleased with him) who said: the Prophet (peace be upon him) said, "Some people of this nation would spend the night dwelling on food and drink and play, and when they wake up in the morning, they find themselves mutated into monkeys and pigs, while earth swallowed the ground under their feet and stones pelted them from heaven. When they arise, they say tonight the earth has swallowed the tribe of so-and-so and the house of so-and-so. They will be pelted with stones from heaven, just as they were sent upon the people of Lot. All this because they took to drinking, supported female singers, devoured usury, and severed the ties of kinship."[78]

---

[77] Musnad Isahac bn Rahweah
[78] Found in Musnad Abi Dawid Al Telsei

BENEVOLENCE TOWARDS PARENTS

It was narrated that Abu Bakra said that the Prophet (peace be upon him) said, "No act of benevolence is apt to be rewarded without delay than fostering the ties of one's kinship. The people of some house may be indecent but, nonetheless, their wealth would grow and their number multiply when they foster the ties of kinship."[79]

It was narrated that Sulayman ibn Amer said that he said, "O Messenger of Allah, my father used to be benevolent to his relatives, fulfill his obligations, and be generous to guests." He said, "He died before embracing Islam?" He said, "Yes." He said, "It will be of no avail to him, but it will benefit his descendants: his sons; you will never be disgraced or humiliated, and you will never get poor."[80]

THE END

---

[79] Ibn Hiban
[80] Couldn't find the source

ABOUT THE AUTHOR

Imam Ibn Qayyim Al-Jawziyya (1292–1350 CE / 691 AH–751 AH)

He was born in Damascus in 691H most scholars of the time have acknowledged the author's excellence, and profound knowledge of Quranic interpretation, commentaries on the prophetic traditions, and theology. His extensive knowledge and understanding of Quranic commentaries surpassed even some renowned theologians in Islamic history.

He is the most outstanding student of Shaikh-ul-Islaam Ibn Taimiyyah, may Allah have mercy on all of them. And work hard on protecting his teacher writings and save them.

After Ibn Taimiyyah dead he starts teaching, and he has many students who became famous Scholars Example Ibn Rajab..

www.ingramcontent.com/pod-product-compliance
Lightning Source LLC
Chambersburg PA
CBHW030913170426
43193CB00009BA/834